WOMEN OF MYTHOLOGY

GODDESSES, WARRIORS, AND HUNTERS

PANDORA

Jodyanne Benson

Cavendish Square
New York

Published in 2020 by Cavendish Square Publishing, LLC
243 5th Avenue, Suite 136, New York, NY 10016

First Edition

Library of Congress Cataloging-in-Publication Data

Names: Benson, Jodyanne, author.
Title: Pandora / Jodyanne Benson.
Description: First Edition. | New York : Cavendish Square, 2020. | Series: Women of mythology: goddesses, warriors, and hunters | Includes bibliographical references and index.
Identifiers: LCCN 2019008837 (print) | LCCN 2019015688 (ebook) |
ISBN 9781502651471 (ebook) | ISBN 9781502651464 (library bound) |
ISBN 9781502651440 (pbk.) | ISBN 9781502651457 (6 pack)
Subjects: LCSH: Pandora (Greek mythological character)--Juvenile literature.
Classification: LCC BL820.P23 (ebook) | LCC BL820.P23 B46 2020 (print) | DDC 398.20938/02--dc23
LC record available at https://lccn.loc.gov/2019008837

Editor: Kristen Susienka
Copy Editor: Alex Tessman
Associate Art Director: Alan Sliwinski
Designer: Christina Shults
Production Coordinator: Karol Szymczuk
Photo Research: J8 Media

The photographs in this book are used by permission and through the courtesy of:
Cover Heritage Images/Getty Images; p. 4 Encyclopaedia Britannica/UIG/Getty Images; p. 6 Matias En ElMundo/iStockphoto.com; p. 7 Universal History Archive/UIG/Getty Images; p. 8 Print Collector/Getty Images; p. 12 DEA Picture Library/Getty Images; p. 14 Mlenny/Getty Images; p. 16 Encyclopaedia Britannica/UIG/Getty Images; p. 18 Heritage Images/Getty Images; p. 19 ZU_09/Getty Images; p. 20 World History Archive/Alamy Stock Photo; p. 22 National Gallery of Art, Washington DC, USA/Bridgeman Images; p. 23 Andrew Harrer/Bloomberg/Getty Images; p. 25 AF Archive/Alamy Stock Photo; p. 27 Ann Ronan Pictures/Print Collector/Getty Images.

Printed in the United States of America

TABLE OF CONTENTS

This drawing shows Pandora opening a jar filled with scary things.

CHAPTER ONE

PANDORA'S JAR

Has your curiosity ever led to trouble? A woman named Pandora caused a lot of trouble because of her curiosity. Let's learn about her story and its lessons for today.

The Myth of Pandora

In Greek mythology, Pandora was the first woman on Earth. Her story begins with a god of fire. His name was Prometheus.

This illustration shows Prometheus bringing fire to humans.

Prometheus was in charge of making men on Earth. He later stole fire from the gods. He gave that fire to men. This angered Zeus, who was the ruler of the gods. He decided to punish Prometheus. Zeus told the god Hephaestus to make Pandora out of the earth. Hephaestus was the god of fire and **craftsmen**.

The **Olympian** gods each gave a gift to Pandora. For example, Aphrodite, the goddess of love, gave her beauty. Zeus

HESIOD'S STORY OF PANDORA

This drawing of Hesiod is from 1825.

Hesiod was a Greek poet. He was the first person to tell the story of Pandora. Her story appears in two of his poems. The first poem is called the *Theogony*. It's an instructional poem. An instructional poem teaches a lesson. These lessons are often about making good choices. Her story also appears in his poem *Works and Days*. *Theogony* and *Works and Days* are both **epics**. Epics are long poems with extraordinary characters. His poems may have been part of an **oral tradition**. This means people told others the stories. People remembered them through the years and eventually wrote them down.

Zeus is often shown riding a chariot. He is the god of sky and thunder in Greek mythology.

told Prometheus's brother Epimetheus to marry Pandora.

Zeus also gave Pandora a jar filled with terrible things. He warned her never to open it. However, soon Pandora became curious about the jar and opened it. When she opened the jar, terrible things escaped—like diseases. The terrible things hurt humans.

Pandora quickly tried to close the jar. Only one thing stayed inside—hope. This is the possibility that something good could happen.

Jar or Box?

In the sixteenth century, Pandora's "jar" became a "box." It is believed that a man named Desiderius Erasmus changed the Greek word for "jar" to "box." Today, most people call it a box.

ANOTHER STORY: EVE

A story similar to Pandora's happens in the Bible with the story of Adam and Eve. In it, God made the first man, Adam. God felt bad that Adam was alone, so God used a rib from Adam's side to make Eve. Eve became Adam's wife. They lived together happily in a beautiful garden called Eden. God told them not to touch the tree of knowledge of good and evil. One day, a snake told Eve that God feared that Adam and Eve would become like him if they ate from the tree. Eve decided to eat one of the tree's fruits. She shared it with Adam. They felt embarrassed and hid. God knew what they did and told them to leave the garden. God also warned them that life from that moment on would be very hard for them and for all humans.

The Myth's Message

The myth of Pandora was very important to the Greeks. It explained how the world became what we see today and helped people understand why bad things existed. It was also a warning about curiosity. Sometimes curiosity can get us into trouble. We might find out more than we can handle.

This drawing shows what Greek life might have been like.

CHAPTER TWO

WOMEN AND MYTHS

Do you ever wonder why certain things happen? Do you wonder why people get sick? What about why there are floods? Well, so did the Greeks! The Greeks told stories to explain the world.

The Stories of Ancient Greece

The **ancient** Greeks believed in gods and goddesses. The gods and goddesses had

The Parthenon temple in Athens, Greece, is dedicated to the Greek goddess Athena.

special powers. Sometimes they were good. Sometimes they were mean. The ancient Greeks built temples to honor them. They also told stories about the gods and goddesses. These stories are called myths. The collection of these myths is Greek mythology. These stories have been told for more than two thousand years.

Myths from ancient Greece are not very different from myths from other **cultures**.

Myths helped people understand the world. The world was a mysterious place to them. These great stories explained things that didn't make sense. They even explained how the world was made.

Myths are much more than made-up stories. Myths tell us about the beliefs of a group of people. They also tell us about gods, goddesses, and events that are important to them.

Women in Mythology

Most women did not have many rights in ancient Greece. They could not vote or own land. Their responsibility was taking care of the home. A few women were able to become poets, philosophers, and artists. They also often appeared in stories and myths.

Athena, the goddess of wisdom, was very powerful. Other important goddesses included Demeter and Persephone. Greeks worshipped these goddesses because they believed they helped food and plants grow. The Muses were also celebrated by the Greeks. They were beautiful and good at art and music.

In Greek mythology, Athena was the goddess of war, crafts, and wisdom.

Like Pandora, many other female characters were troublemakers in myths. These myths actually teach us a lot about men in ancient Greece. Why were women often villains in these stories? Women were givers of life. However, ancient Greeks did not understand how life began. It was a big mystery. Women were seen as very powerful, but this mystery of life also made people afraid of them.

Athens and Theater

Athens was a major city in ancient Greece. People who lived there wrote some of the world's first plays. The plays were performed in a large, outdoor theater.

WOMEN IN ANCIENT GREECE

The myth of Pandora makes us wonder what life was like for women in ancient Greece. Pandora was created to punish Prometheus. The Greek myths often showed women as weak and sneaky. Men were seen as responsible for controlling women. They needed to keep the women from causing trouble. This is why women worked inside the home. They were not seen as important enough to work in schools or government. Men also wrote many of these popular myths. This leads to an important question: What do you think women in ancient Greece thought of themselves?

This jar shows the goddess Aphrodite.

Pandora was not the only woman in myths to cause problems. Helen of Troy caused the Trojan War. Hera could not control her jealousy. By the fifth century BCE, women were given better roles. They started to appear in stories as **heroines**.

Helen of Troy was said to be the most beautiful woman in Greece.

An Important Place

Athens became the world's first democracy. This means that male Athenians could choose their leaders. However, women still didn't have a lot of rights.

Art and statues of Pandora have been created throughout history. This marble statue was made by John Gibson in the nineteenth century.

CHAPTER THREE

PANDORA FOR TODAY

Pandora is still popular today. She has inspired artists and poets all over the world. Her myth also teaches important lessons. Let's learn about where you can see Pandora today.

Pandora in Paintings

Many artists have painted Pandora. Some artists show the effects of her actions.

Other artists imagine Pandora's story differently. The French painter Odilon Redon lived in the 1800s and 1900s. One of his paintings of Pandora shows the moment when Pandora is deciding whether to open the box. Redon painted Pandora very big. The box is in the center of the painting. Redon wanted to show Pandora's interest in the box. This part of the story was important to Redon. Other artists, like Dante Gabriel Rossetti, explored other parts of Pandora's story.

Odilon Redon made this painting of Pandora around 1910.

Beyond the "Box"

Today, businesses are naming themselves "Pandora." One example is Pandora Radio. It's an internet music company. People can listen to endless songs using Pandora. Listeners can click on a thumbs up for songs they like and thumbs down for songs they don't like. Pandora then plays more songs that it thinks the listener will like.

Pandora Radio is the Pandora's box of music. Music lovers

Pandora Radio finds endless songs for you to like or skip based on your musical tastes.

can't wait to hear their next favorite song played. They're curious to know the song that will play next.

Lessons for Today

Can you believe a story from so long ago is still important today? The myth of Pandora tells us a lot about people's weaknesses. It also describes why humans act the way we do. Sometimes when we know we can't have something, we want it even more.

Saturn's Moon

Moons of the planet Saturn are named after myths. One of these moons was named Pandora in 1985. It's very icy and shaped like a potato.

TV AND PANDORA'S BOX

The *Hotel Transylvania* TV show is based on the movie with the same name.

Television shows and movies today are still mentioning popular myths from long ago. Why? These myths are great stories! They still teach important lessons. The Disney Channel television show called *Hotel Transylvania: The Series* has an episode about Pandora's box. The series follows the adventures of Mavis and her monster friends. In one episode, Mavis and her friends try to open Pandora's box. Everyone wants to know what's inside. What do you think happens once it's opened? The ending turns out a little funnier than the myth!

However, it's often in our best interest to obey. Even today, you might hear someone warn you about "opening a Pandora's box." What they mean is that you should think before investigating something you are unsure about. It might not be worth the trouble.

This myth was important for another reason in ancient times. It explained why

Myths, Fables, and Folktales

Myths are stories that explain the world. Fables are short tales with real or made-up animals that act like humans. Folktales are stories about a legend, lesson, or hero from a certain culture.

This painting shows Pandora after she opens the box. She looks innocent rather than dangerous.

bad things happen in the world. The ancient Greeks wondered a lot about what happened around them. They didn't understand why people got sick. They didn't know why nature was so random and mysterious. Explanations like Pandora's story made the world a little less scary—even if they weren't true.

GLOSSARY

ancient Old, or from a long time ago.

craftsmen Highly skilled workers.

cultures Beliefs and customs shared by a group of a people in a certain time and place.

epics Long, story-like poems that describe the adventures of mythological characters and heroes.

heroines Female heroes.

Olympian One of the ancient Greek gods living on Mount Olympus.

oral tradition The collection of stories that people share by telling them to one another.

FIND OUT MORE

Books

Hamilton, Edith. *Mythology*. New York, NY: Black Dog & Leventhal, 2017.

Napoli, Donna Jo. *Treasury of Greek Mythology*. Washington, DC: National Geographic, 2014.

Website

***National Geographic Kids*: Ancient Greek Myths**

www.natgeokids.com/nz/discover/history/greece/greek-myths

Video

Greek Mythology for Kids: Pandora's Box

www.youtube.com/watch?v=8cqvbMr_2mQ

INDEX

Page numbers in **boldface** refer to images. Entries in **boldface** are glossary terms.

ABOUT THE AUTHOR

Jodyanne Benson is a writer and editor from Wisconsin. A longtime teacher, Benson believes that great books spark wonder, curiosity, and learning. She enjoys reading and spending time with her family.